One of the king's helpers, Haman, hated Mordecai because Mordecai would not bow down to him?

DID YOU KNOW...
Haman convinced King Xerxes to make a law that Mordecai and all the Jewish people should be killed?

DID YOU KNOW...
King Xerxes did not know that his beautiful young queen was a Jewish girl?

DID YOU KNOW...
When Mordecai heard the new law, he sent a message to Queen Esther, asking her for help?

DID YOU KNOW...
Even though he had not called for her and she might be punished, Esther bravely went to see the king?

DID YOU KNOW...
Esther invited the king and Haman to a banquet, and there she told the king that Haman wanted to destroy her people?

DID YOU KNOW...

King Xerxes was angry with Haman and told Esther to make a new law to save the Jewish people?

Esther's bravery and trust in God were part of God's plan to keep his people safe in Persia.